CONVERSATION
WITH A
STONEMASON

Also by D. H. Melhem

POETRY

Notes on 94th Street
Rest in Love
Children of the House Afire/More Notes on 94th Street
Country: An Organic Poem
Poems for You

PROSE

Blight: A Novel
Gwendolyn Brooks: Poetry and the Heroic Voice
Heroism in the New Black Poetry
Reaching Exercises: The IWWG Workshop Book

MUSICAL DRAMA

Children of the House Afire

EDITOR

Mosaic: Poems from an IWWG Workshop
A Different Path: An Anthology of RAWI
(with Leila Diab)

CONVERSATION
WITH A
STONEMASON

Poems by

D. H. Melhem

IKON
New York, New York

Some of these poems have appeared in the following publications: *Al Jadid, American Poetry Anthology, Ararat, Central Park, Confrontation, Croton Review, The East Hampton Star, Forkroads, The Formalist, Gargoyle, Graffiti Rag, Home Planet News, Light, The Literary Review, Medicinal Purposes, The New Press, The New York Times, NOW-NYC News, Paintbrush, Pivot, Poetry in Performance 24, 25, 26, 27, 30, Poets for Africa, Rattapallax, The Smith, Snake Pit City, Time Capsule, Valhalla 6, The Women's Record, The WREE-View, Whelks Walk Review.* "Riverside" is published in *Poetrybay,* an internet magazine.

Several poems have been published in *Grapeleaves: A Century of Arab American Poetry* (University of Utah Press, 1988; Interlink, 2000). "To My Unknown Sister in Beirut," first printed in *And Not Surrender: American Poets on Lebanon* (Arab American Cultural Foundation, 1982), is slightly modified here. Of the "Requiescant" cycle, "September 11, 2001, World Trade Center, Aftermath," appears in *The World Healing Book* (Beyond Borders, Iceland, 2002). The poem has been excerpted on a quilt by Liz Cenedella, inscribed on an accompanying plaque by Bob Cenedella, and travels with the quilt to international exhibitions.

To all the above, grateful acknowledgment is made.

ISBN: 0-945368-07-0
First Edition
Library of Congress Control Number: 2003101035

IKON
151 First Avenue, #46
New York, NY 10003
IkonInc@aol.com

CONTENTS

Heritage

Elegiac

Poems to My Former Husband

Art

Convergences

AUTHOR'S PREFACE

Although the somewhat protean concept and content of this book trace growth and change over the years, it was not until my writer's residency at the Château de Lavigny, Switzerland, that the manuscript emerged in its final configuration. The ambience created by my fellow writers and our hostess in an exquisite Alpine setting eased the task. I thank Susan Tiberghien for her special kindness and interest, Pat Carr for urging me to apply, and Hannelore Hahn, whose International Women's Writing Guild illumines and affirms life. I am indebted also to the entire Committee of the Ledig-Rowohlt Foundation, and to the benign shades of Jane and Heinrich Maria Ledig-Rowohlt, who continue to inspire their literary children. Susan Sherman's support has been invaluable.

The essence and the fortitude of my fellow New Yorkers fill me with awed humility, and no small measure of pride.

New York City, 2003

for Dana, Gregory, George

and to the memory of

My Mother and Father

Chester

Aunt Jerry

SELF NOTES

SUNRISE

O! the one Life within us and abroad . . .
          —Samuel Taylor Coleridge, "The Eolian Harp"

Coming up fast
lifting your bitter edges
                    day   day
squirm through cracks of
consciousness
its worn shoes
their smell   of old promenades

RIVERSIDE PARK

Time spaces:
clouds and smoke
walkers and riders, backs
dwindling into landscape,
those on the left, advancing
along fences, their time,
before buildings, their time,
with levels of people in them,
separately pacing.

Gulls like ducks float downriver. A boat
sails through its time.
One crabapple, unattained,
prolongs its season
on a topmost branch.
I too hold on
to images:

A pigeon's walk, how the head
dips forward at each step
that seeks the grass, how
its brown-and-white
feathers are patched
with purple, how the trees
align between breezes,
how a man, crash helmeted,
rides his bike, and a woman
on roller skates
moves in kneepads and armpads
toward a bench; how trust
settles here, in the sun,
on a promenade
reasonably smooth.

Bike rider pauses
to straddle the stone lookout,
and a woman, leashed dogs,
litter paper in hand (before
the public benches),
unleashes farther on.

Paddle ball on the lawn divider.
To my conceptual eye:
the sphere
permanently in air.

Late afternoon coolness
draws through the leaves
another time.

JAPANESE MAPLE BEFORE WINTER

Bleeds its leaves
in a circle.

Four iron fan chairs
backs turned
attend
a round slate table.

Grass rake claws
the stain.

Minutes
(or years)
fall measureless
from an oval sky.

NAKED WOMAN WALKS DOWN THE STREET
for B., E., and G.

majestic
a living statue
with a train of curious children
who crown her with laughter
and shrieks. Before she
rounds the corner to be plucked
into a police car, I see her lead
an army of homeless people who rise up from Penn
Station
and Grand Central and the Port Authority Bus Terminal
and the next block. And the woman is clothed
in rainbow and light from hummingbird wings.
Her followers turn to moving stone and bronze.
They drop off in ones and twos
along Broadway, stationing themselves
at the head of subway stairs.
Their hands are raised and their fists are clenched.
Their stone and bronze children are pointing.
One cannot run past without touching them.
The touch is electric
to feel those statues—
their malice, their might.

ON THE HOMELESS PEOPLE OF NEW YORK CITY

People in houses
can be hard
as the plaster walls
that wall them in,
hard as the oak
they walk upon,
hard as the metal
doors they close.

They close their doors
on the ragged street
on the homeless ones
who bear the smell
of a deadly cold
or a deadly heat
and the weight of shopping bags
crammed with defeat.

THRIFT SHOP BLUES

This was your shirt, Mr. K.
Nearly new, gray-striped Egyptian cotton,
with lightly starched white collar.
Do you throw away shirts after
one or two wearings? (The rich
are mostly thrifty.)
Was it an extravagance?
Did you die and your family couldn't
bear to see your things around?

"Such beautiful shirts!" cried Daisy
to Gatsby, with tears recalled from
the faded silks of night. Would you have
hated tears and stiffened the decorum
into which you were finally poured?
Would you have gibed (unlike Gatsby),
"No crocodile tears"? A river
can taste bitter
when you breathe it.

Maybe you just got tired of
snapping the collar shut
after buttoning seven buttons,
tired of the temporal mischief
of details.

HEART TROUBLE, FOR OUR HOMER, AT SEVENTEEN

Heart trouble,
the vet said—meaning
you loved much
and it harmed you?—
that abyss where we would disappear
and you lived
a dire expectancy?
Were the restorations
as difficult
as the losses?

Only a shadow
moves in your
milky eyes
yet you follow
my feet, and my voice
reaches you
in the smell of dinner
or a soft pat.

You are eluding me
into old photographs.

Fearing the next step
you bump into walls,
limp from one side of the hall
to the other, mapping it
ad hoc.

I must catch you
even as your image
slips out of my arms
to a country road
bright with dogscent,
squirrels, dogwood,
and a whiff of the sea.

HOLIDAY LOSSES

A stained glass holly leaf, its berry a tear,
tiny velvet stockings edged with lace,
a plastic moon lean against the bookcase
strung with greeting cards aligning the year
on threads weighted with annual joy or fear,
with losses and whatever leaves a trace
of longing. Light from the sky, a blank, snow face
threatens and promises like a parent, severe
yet loving. Dim light drops from a little tree
that, walled in a pot, roots toward water and earth
to tap a wider nourishment, where the past
runs, rumbles lightly, clear, and free.
Miniature compresses death and birth;
each year grows smaller, smaller than the last.

FRIENDS

People we cry to are important:
they cradle our consciousness
they embrace our midnights
they pull back curtains of moonlight
and deliver fragile stars

TEACHING ENGLISH COMPOSITION

For a recurrent hour this room
redeems the individual past, collects
its future.

On the blackboard: "Good morning" in
Spanish, French, Gaelic, Greek,
Yoruba, Hebrew, Arabic
daily translates that
English is just one lesson.

THE USE OF LITERATURE

every good heart must stop /
                              at last
thoughts that issue
will falter
the careful folders my files
not grow

must put myself
in order

past at my pen
present on paper
have been well-used by my life
to tell you

CULTURAL EXCHANGES

ADAPTATION

His name is John E. Allen. He is an actor, endowed
with charm, intelligence, attraction, and one of the
realities of his existence is being a dwarf. I met him at
a neighborhood bar; we were seated together on stools.
He told me about his life in England, where he was born.
He told me of his normal-sized family and what it was
like to grow up different. The indifference of girls was
hard. He felt sorry for himself until he was taught to
swim by a man with no arms or legs. He sews his own
clothes. He is writing the biography of a late actor, also a
dwarf, so that people might understand such lives. I said
the story would be universal; not all handicaps could be
seen. He told me he got stuck writing sometimes, and I
offered to help. He took my card. Before tucking it into
his shirt pocket, he folded it in half.

BORDELLO

Hooked
girlbody
thick hands reel in
your silicone-breasted years
bobbing on waves of
red damask

AMBITION

you said: Africa
opportunity for
a mercenary
I thought you said
a missionary

life light and death
are clearly mixed
in you

SMOKE

That one time, newly, you took me by your firm hand
its pulse tingling my fingertips
we ran down Broadway
up creaky stairs to
the billiard parlor
a world of mossy islands
spattered with billiard balls and crossed
with cue sticks, the rosin of concentration,
lampshades and eyeshades and
men leaning into smoke
measuring their shots
oh, the green world of then
as I aimed
you guiding my hand respectfully
as if it might be
a green hand for a new life
and a place to stay.

                         Women
took you in. Women
tasted your sweetness
as you sucked at the nipples
of chance.
                 Boy-man,
the game turns
grotesque.
In worn heels, torn pockets,
a sweater unraveling
against necklace of
OTB tickets, your sole victory is
the new girl at the bar.

Boy-man,
smoke your dreamy dreams
into erections
smoke your dreamy dreams
out of this world into yourself
you keep getting smaller
rolling your bones
into joints of thin paper
smoke your dreamy dreams
boy-man, as you grow old.

CULTURAL EXCHANGE

Plaiting your hair
at bedtime
half-expecting to achieve
a child's image
I discover
an African warrior:
sturdy wisps braided
over the patience
that gives your mild expression
its power
eyes hiding partly
a knowledge behind them
nostrils flared
and the lips
their savor of plums
held finely.

In the morning
you release the bunched tips.
A black crown attends
your body of ancient legends.

ATHLETE

It is the shoulder touches me, the one
dislocated in football—not the cleat mark
on your nose or the scar on your arm
or the birthmark/burn on your leg
but the fragility of that frame
so wisely knit so
perfectly detailed
for speed

IN PART

Because I do not wish to love I love
your eyes your ears the soft hair
in your armpits your drawl the deep
tones of your flesh the rim of your knees
your nose your toes your sex your ideas and never
put these together
allinone

YOUNG LOVER

What shall I do with this young girl in me
when you will see my years under my wild hairs
and run from them as from Medusa?
Where shall I take this me
that does not falter or tire,
sunlit, strong, loving you?

To the deep image of myself
rid of its skin of time
so fiercely inscribed
with those who have loved me
in however partial or impermanent a style.

PERCUSSIONIST

1

Conga drum bongo drum
your arms and fingers hit them
caress them draw their turbulence
through our bodies that sway
into their shuddering air.

Hit it true.

Your face bends over them
like a source of drums
issuing from your eyes
behind smoked lenses.

Hit it, *mmmmmmmm.*

Your lips move
and your smile discloses
recognitions of right sounds
at precise times
that formulate
a rumbling power
that may
thread the shimmering
triangle into a shower
of high sounds
floating down into the drums
the pools of them, reflecting
your intense face, nightshine,
controlling ecstasy.

Hit it free.

2

Although my heart has not been
tempered by the same
drums out there
or the saxophone at the same
moment of childhood that adheres
to the back of the head
I am still something with it
part of it rattling shhhh rocking me
rumbling into my poemmmmm
shrilling my eloquent blood
past grim labyrinthine games that
departmentalize me
this is a way out
for my spirit
to mombo my leaping
negatives out out the door to you
who beat the drum groan
d/d/drummmmm
around me the arms of your drums
that move my body open to kiss
the rings of your
muuuuusic

3

fingers like
whirring wings of light from Nassau coral
black pearl moonbeam sea my ear is
close ah close to sand I hear through
cellar of this sky a hummingbird
the burnished green flowing through
your eyes a sunlight through these lines
that follow tone and timbre of you
toes that heed your heart rippling out your hands
to the drum   the drum that feels you happy
sends the lyric of your spirit   into my song

MEXICAN DIVER, ACAPULCO, ON TV

I, too, high diver
go down
back arched
as if head up
I might rise
continue the curve
of a parabolic gesture
to will the going

ON YOUR WAY TO TUNISIA
for N. L., entering the Peace Corps

When you span the Atlantic
and your plane zooms past Gibraltar
toward the Tunisian airport,
when the Africa of your mind
turns to dusty pavement under your shoes
and the gleaming images of the Mediterranean
touch your cheek with ancient breezes,
unpack your suitcases into
hammada and kalaa,
caves and plains and mountain valleys,
Aleppo pines and evergreen oaks,
juniper and wild olive and pistachios,
fauna and reptiles and fish,
unpack into oases,
into Berbers and Matmatas and Muslims,
Moors and Christians and Jews,
into Tunis and Sfax and Sousse,
archaic Phoenicia and Carthage
and failed colonial regimes,

contagious terrains
of possibilities.

*hammada—rock-floored or rock-strewn desert region,
    especially in the Sahara*
kalaa—plateaus with abrupt sides

HERITAGE

FOR THE LEBANON, SYRIA, AND GREECE IN MY AMERICAN SELF

Love song, go to my history:
to the Lebanese teachers and Syrian merchants
Greek physicians and warriors for independence
singers and chanters and poets
perfumers and dealers in lumber and grain—
to the high music of an ancient tongue
glistening its golden gutturals
among tears and persistence
that string the oud and beat the durbakkah
from continent to continent
and curve round the drums of our
brothers and sisters in spirit and music—
durbakkah and oud.
Dance your coils of dark hair,
dance your circles of hands.
Sparks fly from your fingertips
to the fallen ones crowding
the walls of the sky.
Durbakkah, durbakkah,
dance with your family the world
and tremble the earth
with the rhythms of justice!

PLAIN STRING

Thanksgiving evening. I have just wiped
a few plates left to drain; I wipe them
clean of spots, they sparkle. And I remember
you, Grandmother, carefully drying
the spoons we had quick-dried
after holiday dinner,
how you studied each spoon for dampness
that might blemish it,
how you sought to impose
on the plain order of your life
perfection, an Aristotelian sense
of ideal form and purpose.

And these causes, your humble act instructed
in other tasks: basting stitches were to be
small and even, before a final sewing,
so that even the things unseen
might leave their aura of excellence.
I remember the string full of knots;
a peculiar chore to untie them.
A work of patience. I learned it.
And then the reward:

cat's cradle—forms
for their own sake.
The white string, the depth of line,
the quick twist into
simplicity, both of us holding it.
That I could share with you something fine,
designing the air into epiphanies!

String, an instrument,
four hands to conduct and orchestrate
with filaments and webs and geometries
together, together not only our hands to their
single tasks, but joined now in dialogue.
You speak, then I speak.
Our language of plain string.

GRANDFATHER: FRAILTY IS NOT THE STORY
for Dana and Gregory

Remember your grandfather tall and straight
Remember him swimming in deep water
Remember his stories of exile and travel
          and immigrant dreams
Remember his ship models designed from memory
Remember him netting shiners with you in Gardiner's Bay
          or digging for clams
          or cleaning a fish
          or driving us fast
          to catch the sunset at Maidstone

I remember him climbing the stairs
          after all the stairs he had climbed
          with his satchel of fabrics
I remember him on stepladders in the Depression
          or holding my hand on the way to school
          me proud of him in his overalls
I remember watching for him at six o'clock
          he would lift me at the door
and then we would sit over roast lamb shanks or chicken
while my mother related the family news.
Afterwards he rose to "stretch his legs,"
          read the paper, and doze.

And I remember discussions, the arguments over politics
          how he taught me to reason, to wield logic
          as he had done when captain of the debating team
          in Tripoli Boys' School, Lebanon
          and the photos of him there, where he was becoming
          the tallest and handsomest man in the town.

I remember the pipes arrayed like sentinels on a cabinet
the talk of building or buying a boat
explanations of algebra (which I learned to enjoy)
and the excursions—
       walking over Brooklyn Bridge into Chinatown
       walking down Ocean Parkway to Sheepshead Bay
or later in a Ford, the three of us, singing
       of the San Fernando Valley
       where we would settle down
       and never more roam.

Remember your grandfather
in his vigor
and that a loving life
takes imagination.

AUNT JERRY

I

Midway between earth and heaven
you chat with the dead.
Last sister, last daughter,
they've come to rescue you
from pills, commodes, bedpans,
from nurses, enemas, pain
stabbing your hands and feet.
You cannot stand, so they lift you—
mother, sisters, brothers,
lift you high above bedsheets.
How light you are! they say.

II

Before I was born, you walked with my mother.
After my birth, you rocked my cradle.
Later you learned
to inch down the stairs
with me in your lap.
I grew up more sister than niece,
more friend than a sister.

III

When Uncle Henry came courting Aunt Rose
we made fudge in the kitchen or escaped
to ice cream in Flatbush.
You liked to repeat, "I'm American!"
though you meant Anglo-Saxon or French,

not a smudge from Mersin
hard to wipe clean
with citizenship papers.
You anglicized your name,
married an Englishman who died young.
A widow, your worked, you traveled.
Anointed company hostess,
you greeted foreign visitors. Retired,
still smoked your pack a day,
then stopped too late.

IV

You were an American.
Even your plastic hangers
were red, white, and blue.
You moved to Latino rhythms,
wore scarlet, revered
Edith Piaf and Charles Trenet.
You taught me the foxtrot,
the rumba, the tango.
I loved your clothes. They always
went dancing at night.

V

Scatter my ashes! Scatter them
between Ellis Island and the Statue of Liberty.
Welcome to New York Harbor.

BEIRUT AND THE UPRISING (1982, ff.)

To My Unknown Sister in Beirut

Sister unknown sister
your voice reaches me
from cedars shrouded
in the rubble of your house
and from your thirsty streets
that drink blood
and bake bodies
like loaves of flat bread
tossed into the sun

Sister unknown sister
our fearful brother brings bombs
our brother who bought death
from my father
our brother who ate the blood-lust
of his tormentors
He ate their defeat
and they took his victory

And the song of his fighter jets
screams   screams
the voices of children who were singing
a people proud to be peaceful

Sister unknown sister
whose dark eyes shadow my escape
are the olives bitter
in your throat?
Their pits embarrass
the politicians
your innocence
the politicians
your agony
the politicians
Sister my sister
there are lessons
to be learned
from death

Boy In A Hospital

Boy in a hospital
lying among suddenly ancient ruins
that join the Temple of Jupiter
at Baalbek
to the gutted apartments
of Beirut
its buildings glutted
with collapsing life
with bodies
like fragments of statues
newly classical

Boy in a hospital
your olive skin has the pallor of smoke
you have had your moment's attention
there is no sanctuary here there is panic here
the wounded are wounded again

How black your eyes stare into the world
that tore from you
mother father sister brother
tore off your legs

There was no food or water
the walls kept going down
the burning sky kept falling

Boy in a hospital
you are the way to Beirut
the road of pain
the road of shouting corpses
of amputated legs thrown into the street
with newspapers and expectations

to dance the dabke
to share your sister's and brother's laughter
rushing up the stairs
to your apartment
to taste your mother's stuffed grape leaves
from the enamel pot
to run along the beach
your hand safely in your father's

Shebab

We do not want bread—we want freedom.
We are men, not animals. We are human beings.
　　　　—One of the Palestinian shebab
　　　　　(young men), interviewed on TV.

Shebab, these stones
hurl their little cries.
You break them from your bloody flesh.
They come out of your houses and hearts.
They drizzle defiance on barbed wires.

You say you have nothing to lose.
Daily the wind that drifts your youth
across Gaza and Sinai
whirls it around minarets
and issues from the mouths of muezzins.

Each stone transforms your graves
into hailstones.

For The Palestinian People

On what map are the footsteps of the Palestinian people?
People of the new diaspora: Where are your armaments
now?

Our footsteps are the earth of Palestine.
Our armaments are our sturdy hearts.

Where are the poems for the Palestinian people?
Poems like rocks from the fractured plateau?
Poems like cool water from a goatskin bag?

Our poetry is breath
like the wind from Gaza to Jordan
from the sea to the Golan Heights
breath that is constant as
a prayer traveling to the stars.

Where are your monuments, O Palestinian people?
Do they lie in the rubble of Beirut?

We take our monuments with us, friend.
We are the monuments, now.

ELEGIAC

MUSEUM CROSSINGS

I

To the mummy of Harwa, storekeeper
in the Temple of Amun at Karnak,
who stands encased within a glass case,
head and wrappings blackened by
the oils and unguents intended to keep you
intact for the crossing from which you were intercepted:

a greeting, in shame
for public ruts and spoiling to display
your stone skin taut over bone, X-ray revealing
that you died of unknown causes at twenty-
five or forty (circa 650 B.C.).

Mode of reverence:
remove internal organs, dry them
with natron for 40 days,
wash, oil, stuff the body,
bandage with 400 yards of linen strips,
place the organs in Canopic jars, coat with
hot liquid pine resin, set the corpse
into its coffin. Become this show.

II

The past is clatter clutter.
Have done with it. Forgive forget Mom/Dad;
empty the canisters of retrospect.
No jar holds more value than itself.
Promises, those fly-traps catch
and crunch the sacred beetles of belief.

Religions flip their channels. We
lower or raise (again) dead hemlines, praise gods
of bigger bucks. Ra energy cheers us on.
Isis, Osiris ride the Underground.
                              Beside you, Harwa:
a foot and a hand in a case.
A little boy unwrapped ("perhaps not
by the museum"). No doll—
a boy. Somebody's son. Who worshipped
the sun. Was beloved and filled with trust.
He whose toes did not yet reach his sandaltips
sickened one morning. Horus flew past
his soul, seized it.

III

Behold the young husband
wrapped in burlap. His wife carries his corpse
furtively to burial in their backyard.
Outside Managua, Nicaragua,
a chromogenic colorprint catches
the hacked torso, the grapestem spine,

a foot, an arm, some bones,
and a thin tree trunk overlooking
mountains and water. Still life
set in a landscape. Interspersed:
war. Undocumented aliens
and children fixed in flight at the Mexican border.

Interrogate. Expose.
Unwrap the ritual past to find—
ourselves? Read meanings
in mere skin. See children
who live and die. Witness a man, a woman
who loved. Mountains and water faithfully rise and flow
past colorprints, fear, bodies,
attacks on temples.

*Note: I and II refer to exhibits in the Field Museum
of Natural History, Chicago; III responds to the
Susan Meiselas photography exhibit "Crossings" at
the Chicago Art Institute.*

HECUBA TO HECTOR

Ah, Hector—blood pools thickly in the eyes
and honor, power, prowess blinds with lust!
If not for Pandarus and the gods, this tide
could well have ebbed to foolish origins,
to Paris and Menelaus grappling
in single combat over Helen, ending
the nine-year siege. War is a serpent—
spews venom on the young. Be Hector in peace,
the tamer of horses! Your glittering helmet
trails its golden plume of horsehair,
dazzles the eye, kills mightily with sword
and spear. But helmet, armor, shield will bend,
brave son whom I raised, step by step,
like an eagle climbing the air. Remember
your wife and child. Remember Andromache.
Glory hews a marble bed and serves
a phantom porridge. Little Scamandrius
at each hand of height will curse
his orphan's tears.

             "War is men's business,"
you say. What then is women's? To tend
the funeral pyres and whitened bones? To pluck
the lyres of lamentation? I should have
rent my breasts before they suckled you
or any of my sons. Do not, I pray,
go out to meet Achilles. Fight
from within these walls.

And yet you go—and yet our grief
runs with you
out the gate.

THE WOMAN WHO THREW HER CHILDREN OUT THE WINDOW

"No more may gulls cry at their ears
Or waves break loud on the seashores; ..."
—Dylan Thomas

He said it was too heavy a load for a man—
strapped to three babies when I left for work
to feed us all and keep the car. He parked them
by the window and went down, then fastened
his seat belt, sped abruptly away trailing
slaps and little tears. When I came home,
once more I heard them at the stairs, crying,
and then they stopped to see their weary mother
had not abandoned them.

        A gull screams, hoarse,
"It's time to try their wings."

        I feed them, hug them,
weep the evening light, imagine angels
airborne in the sun. No no I won't
abandon angels joyful in their wings.

"Decide! Decide!" the sky voice calls to me.

I'll mail them up to heaven, to the stars
where they'll shine too, but first
I'll wash their faces, dress them in their best,
so we can go together, one by one.

Maybe in flight we'll glimpse his car or he'll
turn back, amazed to see our glory trail.

FOR DUK KOO KIM, BOXER

When you first traded those punches
happily you jumped up and
clapped your gloves over your head—
you thought you were winning
big bucks in a big fight U.S.A.
world-famous WBA Lightweight Champion
beating Ray (Boom Boom) Mancini
in a life-or-death battle a gamble at Las Vegas,
as you told your mother who waited in Seoul, Korea.

We said, "We'll hold the purse till you climb
out of the ring." Those jabs to your body those blows
to your head unprotected—
you were knocked down counted out carried out
on a stretcher, Mr. Kim. Your life
splattered our canvas. We are crude artists,
Mr. Kim.

FOR ELEANOR BUMPURS, CITIZEN OF NEW YORK CITY

She was a person, too....I demand justice.
—Mary Bumpurs, NBC-TV, April 12, 1985

It took you sixty-six years
to get there
two rooms
in a city project
a piece of sky
you could lock in.
Outside
everybody was the landlord.

Eleanor Bumpurs
your eyes
in newspapers
look away worried—
was it the rent?
the shotguns?

That last October morning
nineteen eight-four
Housing Authority clamored,
"Open up the door!"
Rumor had it
you might fight.
Social worker, expectant
of lye, sniffed disinfectant.

The Emergency Service Squad
ready to handle
a dangerous woman

rode to battle
an anonymous case.

Citizens:
Thank you
for shotguns.
We face the wild ones
with masks
and plastic shields
a six-foot T-bar rod
like a toothless rake.
Sometimes you prod
to pin them against a wall.
She weighed three hundred pounds.
Had lye, they said.
She had a knife. I swear
she came at me.

We need
new weapons
that fire electric shock
after we break the lock.
Maybe we need
new guidelines
to require
hostage-negotiations
before we open fire.

I heard them at the door.
I heard them at the lock.
Lord!
Broke that little door
like they broke my skin.
Two of them rushed in
came at me with the rod.

Mask didn't fool me!
Shield didn't either!
Devil with a pitchfork—
that's who he was.
Jumped up from hell.
Stuck me good.
I raised my sword!

They scared, I hear
cause I'm so big.
Well, a person's a person
no matter how burly
no matter how small
no matter how old
no matter how poor
a person's a person!

Wild things
with no faces
break through your wall
hunting you—
what do you do?
When devil rushes in
I raise a righteous sword!

On the streets
of garbage rot
I will not
put my chair
my kettle my plate
my bed my name.
I am not tame.

When devil rushes in
I raise a righteous sword!

Shot off my hand.
Broke open my chest.
Made me a dead load
for Lincoln Hospital.

In the apartment
somebody quick-mopped
my blood.
My blood held on.
Daughter Mary
found my finger
on the kitchen floor.
Think of it
think of it
pointing.

TO AN ETHIOPIAN CHILD

When you sang the clear water of your mother's womb
she blessed your body with the cry of her thighs.
Strong as a river, she floated you on her stomach,
she floated you on her back. With her hands
she cleft the air clean for your breath.
You were born to the sun, to the opal sky,
to the fig and pomegranate and apricot,
korareema, sansevieria,
to the cotton for your shehma,
to the red blossoms of the Kosso tree,
to the mimosa and myrrh that fragrance you.

Why does the sun yield no day to rain,
beat back grain to the ground?
Your water song gurgles the air.
You drink your tears.
Your mother bleeds milk into your mouth.
She claws the earth
to find you a porridge of mud.

Can you eat your heritage down to the stones?
Can you eat those stones down to bedrock?
Can you chew the baga, the dry season?
Wait for keuramt to come. Wait for monsoon
to anoint the table land.

Your face that lifts from newspapers
looks out at me from TV.
Who is this plucked bird, fly-specked?
Who is this skull on a stick?

Your mother leans from the screen.
She wrenches you from her empty breast

and sets you on my table. Your hand
rests on mine that presses the gravy spoon
into mashed potatoes, leaving a brown pool.
You wait, then slip back
into TV, where
your mother holds you again.
She brushes flies from your open eyes.

The picture flickers with heat, flickers with dust
into a dry assembly of skulls,
increasing,
flickering.

Korareema: Amharic, Ethiopian spice.
Sansevieria: genus of African or Asian herbs; leaves
        sometimes used in making bowstrings, cordage,
        or in packing.
Shehma: Amharic, Ethiopian national cotton dress.
Kosso tree: Ethiopian tree whose fruit had medicinal uses.
Baga: Amharic, Ethiopian dry season (summer,
        September-May).
Keuramt: Amharic, Ethiopian rainy season (winter,
        June-August).

POEMS TO MY FORMER HUSBAND

HOUSEWIVES' REVOLT

I feel with Sara Fricker, knowing
that Coleridge no longer loved her
that he loved another Sarah
of whom he dreamed and wrote
and so when Charles Lamb visited
the lime tree bower, prepared to walk
with Samuel around the lake
as William and Dorothy had done
Sarah spilled the boiling milk
upon her husband's foot.

Tonight at dinner,
you seated, requesting,
I, vexed by servility,
served the chilly canteloupe
to your feet.

DUALISM

As I was walking down the street
        my second self I chanced to meet
I, wife and mother, cook and nurse
        not happier or better, worse
perhaps, for being worn and used
        a trifle hard (though not abused
in any harsh or obvious way)
        just having time denied, deferred
or taught to think myself absurd—
        that second self who would be heard
while learning silence was preferred.

And so the first was given rein
        to mute with goodness private pain—
greet it politely, yet permit
        that self that soul no benefit
of entry, having rejected it.

As I was walking down the street
        my second self I saw retreat
I longed, a moment, to embrace
        the gossamer that trailed my space
but awkward, shy, I missed the pace
        that might redeem discarded grace.

APHASIA

my eyes' intensest images
dissolve
this hospital room

sun on the window
strikes   you recede
into utterance

you seek
a word

metaphors merge
at their edges

you say two things
in one
and one
is another
relations
constant
are there

expression
eludes
all the words
encircle
they surround you
they surround me

you make
a hoop of words
enclosing us

A WINTER LAKE

Someone who loved you young
holds youth in you
with remembering eyes   retains
the point ingeminate
that proud season

I see past whiskers and slackening skin
the set mouth and its mischief
to the cold high sun of a winter's day
over a lake of skaters   how we dared

the thin edge   but in the end
did not advance too far

and though we were not timid
or thought not that we were
we did not   test then
our singleness   but went together
an exchange of hands and blades
toward the chill, indefinite air

RETRIEVAL

old sparring mate old lover
we who have scarred each other
know that battering can also hammer out
a kind of gold, marked and thin
but fine for all that, retaining
something of value, that holds

CHESTER POEMS

I

house blown apart
a part missing

• • •

when you died
pumpkin collapsed
on the front step
car battery died in the driveway
fuse blew in the basement
lights went out
nothing was right in the house
anymore

• • •

you stood at the back door
grip in hand   as if
waiting for a taxi

the inspector
drove up
took you indoors
to inspect you

(if he had should he have
could they have saved you?

volunteer medics
measured
fed pills
you felt worse
in the ambulance

• • •

at the hospital
tube sprouts
grew on your breath

three more days and they had you

II

I keep some close things
put on your skin with gloves
with big socks
your paisley scarf
hugs me

• • •

in the photograph
you wear a uniform
smile your young smile
wartime

• • •

Help! Where is my validation?

• • •

Dead is easy
say the dead
pulling my head down
to the birthing of stars

I swallow
the sweet morning air

• • •

Uncoiling my lungs
you shout
my dreams.

• • •

Your address is mine again.
We merge
in mail
forwarded to now.

• • •

Amaryllis
in a pot
points green
clenches
a ragged bulb.

Blades rise
plump pocket bulges
its bellybud.

• • •

I am at the road, raking leaves.
You stand in the driveway.
We wave.

ART

HONORING MATISSE

1. "On the Terrace, Saint-Tropez"

A young man, no, a pattern, yes, a pattern of
blue-and-white tortoise shell slumps against a wall.
Tree branches detached from the open sky
swirl over him. Orange flowers focus the observer
away from pity, from the young man who flinches
    into place.
He holds white and pink (a baby? a book?) in his lap.
Column, branch, flower, man,
nature morte.

2. "Conversation"

He stands erect in striped pajamas;
stiffly she sits in black.
Two islands on a blue canvas.

Between them, a sly window:
wrought-iron ledge (her pattern, her color),
a tree (his pattern) with a little blue island
projecting from the trunk
(or red fish in a puddle? with autumn leaves
in her silhouette?)

His hands: half-hidden in pockets.
Hers: exposed to the tips.
They stare, they glare.
"The eternal conflict of
drawing and color."
Acts of repression.
You, me.

3. "The Swimming Pool"

"I have always adored the sea, and now that I can no
longer go for a swim, I have surrounded myself with it."
-- Henri Matisse

Blue against white. Cutouts.
Gouache, pasted on
white painted paper
mounted on burlap.

Cut-up!

Rise into starfish, porpoise, gulls.
Liberate the mermaids!

Even when you tread water
you go somewhere.

ON A PAINTING BY WANG MENG (1308-1385), AT THE METROPOLITAN MUSEUM

Ginkgo grasps at
my open window
with fluttering arms arching
into my room, itself a margin of calm where
the quiet borders of my life
summon

the scholar in Wang Meng's "Simple Retreat." He
sits at his front gate
holding a magic fungus
while a servant and two deer approach from the woods.
In the courtyard another servant proffers
a sprig of herbs to a crane.
Rocks and trees, alive in cascading brushstrokes
of dots and washes and daubs of mineral pigment
draw their energy across paper
where green-and-black trees (one orange-leaved)
are swirling about the tranquil rectangles.

In Arles, Van Gogh also
trembled with nature
and painted his life into
star-drenched trees
unfurling their passionate scrolls
onto the night.

Wang Meng, by daylight,
drew existence
to his long view
of the mind
enclosing stability
in a vortex of change.

JACOB LAWRENCE, IN RETROSPECT, AT THE
DETROIT INSTITUTE OF ARTS, April 11, 2002

Far from your studio
in a clear glass case
paint tubes
like fingers
await impulse.

You didn't mix colors,
declared pigments
exactly:

forest green, thalo green,
permanent green light,
olive green,
Kooker's green light.
The reds:
cadmium red deep,
alizarin crimson,
raw siena.
And cobalt blue,
oxide of chromium,
zinc white.

Round tubes—
crying *squeeze me*
onto canvas, onto paper;
powdered paints
in plain jars
with black lids.
Small dishes
for water.

Liberating hues stride
across canvas, across paper.
Small steps carry through
the idea, penciled in
at first, a group,
the whole series,
then one color
at a time
for each segment.
You conceived
the pattern
revealed
like pages.

Design:
Touissaint L'Ouverture,
The Northern Migration,
John Brown,
Frederick Douglass,
Harriet Tubman.
History!
Get it down.

Gradations selected.
Complexities compressed
into stories.

The Hiroshima Series.
Set apart:

Farmers. Family.
People in the Park.
Man with Birds.
Street Scene.
Playground:

Boy looks up at black sky.
Broken
kite lies
on the ground.
Everywhere
crimson faces,
crimson hands
sprouting
white ash.
The dog, too.

All the animals suffered.

At the end,
the Builders Series.
Lasting things.
Artist with tools.
Brushes, hand tools.
Hammer, nails.
In each painting
a box of tools.
Joseph had a carpentry shop.
You said,
"Tools are beautiful."

At the end
there was that
solidity.
Creation.

MOORE-SAN

Moore-san
iron-faced goddess
protecting this house:
I salute you.
Oak trees dip their branches.
Concrete blocks affirm you.
Earth cradles your clay.

Like you I weather
crackle with heat
stand in rainwinds
showered with snow.
The stars shower me too
and pile up around me
like days that are little wrecks
whose debris I try to see through,
but can't. At night
they weight my shoulders
like a shawl of stones

or a spring morning
pressed in a book.

At the school entrance
my mother's hand
releases mine, as if each day
she is carving these steps
for me to rush through
the doors of my future.

Moore-san,
head without body,
base an inverted flower pot
concave eyes
lidless, tears all fallen
out of them:
your look follows me indoors
reminding that journeys are hard.

Hands carefully
guide your features.
It is difficult
to be shaped
out of mud.
You and the sculptor wrestle
to become yourselves.
Only one may survive.

I strive to shape you clearly
within myself.
Your gaze guides my heart
and lets me go.

*"Moore-san" is the name of an iron-oxide-coated clay head
sculpted by Amejo Amyot. The name refers to sculptor Henry
Moore, an influence, and to the Japanese cast of the figure's
countenance. It stands in a Long Island garden.*

VARIATIONS ON A THEME BY ANDREA MANTEGNA

I. "Pallas Expelling the Vices from the Garden of Virtue"[1]

In a garden (not Eve's, not Adam's, but like theirs,
unmarred by history), marked by eleven arches,
four focusing a low lattice fence
that retains rose bushes escaping to climb
and cluster at the top between the curves,
a stone wall on the right defies time,
which enters vigorously from the left:
Pallas Athena, one hand clasping the shaft
of a broken spear; the other raising her shield
against a swarm of armed cupids. Helmeted,
splendid in red, gold, white, and blue, she bursts
through the arch.

                        Clothed and unclothed figures scatter.
Some flee on land; others through stagnant waters
of a swamp moat. Avarice, a lean woman
with spear-like breasts, leads the flight of Vices
through the swamp. She and Ingratitude carry
the fat, crowned figure of Ignorance. Behind them
a satyr clasps an infant and a bearskin.
In the foreground, a monkeylike hermaphrodite,
Immortal Hatred, Fraud, and Malice, looks back
fearfully at Athena, as he clutches
his four seedbags of evil. Idleness,
armless, naked, is pulled along with a rope
by tatterdemalion Sloth. Venus, off-center,
her scant green scarf billowing about her,
stands on the back of a centaur, while ahead,
Cupid raises his torches of love.

Two women in green and blue, who carry a bow
(Diana?) and an extinguished torch (of Chastity?)
lead the approach to Venus. Tall as an arch,
transforming into a tree with upraised branches,
a greenish figure cries to the turbulent sky:
"Come, divine companions of the Virtues,
who are returning to us from Heaven, banish
these foul monsters of vice from our seats."

In a fleecy mandorla of clouds hover
Temperance, who waters down her wine,
Justice, with her scales and sword, and
Fortitude, who holds a column and club
and wears Hercules' lion skin. Below,
immured in the garden wall, Prudence releases
a little banderola, urging, in Latin,
"And you, oh gods, succor me, the mother of virtues."

II. Christopher Columbus

And somewhere in Mantegna's time, Cristoforo Colombo,
a virtuous gentleman of Genoa, was going ashore
in San Salvador, in the Bahamas,
to take possession of Arawak land for Castile.

"To win their friendship, and realizing that here was a
people to be converted to our Holy Faith by love and
friendship and not by force, I gave some of them red caps,
glass beads, and many other little things. These pleased
them very much and they became very friendly. They
later swam out to the ship's boats in which we were
seated, and brought us parrots and balls of cotton and
spears. . . . They willingly traded everything they owned.
But they seemed to me a poor people . . . naked. . . .

Both men and women cried, 'Come and see the men
who have come from heaven, and bring them food and
water.'. . . Should your Majesties command it, all the
inhabitants could be taken away to Castile, or made
slaves on the island." And when the Santa Maria
foundered on a reef off Haiti, Guacanagari, the local
chief or cacique, who had already met Columbus and sent
him presents, including a gold mask, hearing of the
misfortune, wept, "and sent me various of his relatives
to implore me not to grieve, for he would give me
everything he had."[2]

The Santa Maria ran aground on Christmas.
Wrenched, from its wounded timbers honoring
Jesus' mother: Fort Navidad. Arawaks,
newly enslaved, lifted hosannas of pain
into its walls. Columbus planted his sailors
like flags claiming the land for the rulers of Spain.

On the Niña, Columbus gathered the rest of his crew.
He rounded up the sample Arawak slaves
and fired the lombard at the carcass hull
of his foundered ship, the Santa Maria, and set sail.

Across the Atlantic, weather turning cold,
the caravels leaked and shivering prisoners died.
Week after week of anguish staggered on
from phantom shores they thought that they had reached:
the Way, the Truth of passage to the East,
the gilded route to Orient gold, Cathay.

The turbulent journey over, in triumph
Columbus entered Barcelona. Six
surviving Indians walked behind in feathers

and little aprons, walked in the chilly air,
waded through roaring mouths and glittering eyes.

Admiral Columbus, hail! Portugal, Spain,
blessed by the Pope, divided the spoils of the world.

And so unleashed the snarling hunt for gold.
Seventeen ships, with fifteen hundred men
set out to conquer savages. Arrived
at quiet Navidad. And waited. Fearfully
men from the villages of Guacanagari
visited by night, with gifts. The Admiral
learned that the colony men had roamed the island
in gangs, looking for gold and raping the women,
and each of the colony men had been captured and killed.

Now the Indians were made to surrender
their golden ornaments, and every day
they washed the gold dust from the streams, as tribute
to buy a three-month copper coin. Without it
hands were hacked off, and they bled to death.

Their pacification intact, the suicides
began en masse. By 1540, Arawaks
collapsed into archaeology. And still
there was no gold. There was no gold. No gold.

III. Vincennes

> "On July 3, 1988, an American warship shot down
> an Iranian airliner, killing 290 civilians. . . . The
> Pentagon tried to cover the tragic blunder."
> "Sea of Lies," *Newsweek,* July 13, 1992.

Burst into burning blood
came screaming down into the Persian Gulf
and doubly drowned in a sea of lies.
The antiaircraft missiles launched into
a yellow haze of sand from the Arabian desert,
and the combat information center lights
dimmed "like a prison's during an execution."[3]

"I made the proper decision," said Captain Rogers,
retiring to his cabin aboard the Vincennes.

It was hot and the Captain was shaving. The frigate
    Montgomery,
escorting Kuwaiti tankers registered under
the U.S. flag to keep the oil flowing, had spotted
thirteen Iranian gunboats in the Strait of Hormuz,
milling about a Liberian tanker, the Stoval.
Somebody heard "explosions." Captain Rogers,
on orders, sent a helicopter to inspect,
but in addition sent a blast through the klaxon
rushing his crew to man their battle stations,
and moved the ship north to Iranian waters.
Omanis ordered Iranian gunboats to leave.
Omanis ordered the warship Vincennes to leave.

Captain McKenna, chief of surface warfare,
also ordered the Vincennes to leave.
Helicopter trailed the gunboats north,
took antiaircraft fire. The Vincennes
moved north again, engaged Iranian gunboats
within their twelve-mile territorial limit.

Iran Air Captain Mohsen Rezaian
announced to the tower at Bandar Abbas Airport
that he was ready for takeoff. Lifted the plane
into the haze, unknowingly, over the Vincennes.

Wearing his jaunty gold-encrusted cap,
Captain Rogers, flanked by battle managers,
sat upright in the womb of his cockpit
at the darkened combat information center,
the windowless combat information center,
and directed warfare by remote control.
The $400,000,000 Aegis computer,
with its four 42-inch-square screens relaying
to rows of operators, each one studying
an element of the battle monitored
on separate radio consoles, the Aegis computer
can track every aircraft within 300 miles,
identify them as friendly or hostile, display
their direction and speed, rank them by danger.

Flight 655, picked up on radar,
was classified as commercial, but was missed
by the petty officer, on his list. A decision
was passed along, part "friction" mixed with fear.[4]

Innocent aircraft in ascent
perceived as hostile, in descent.
Two SMZs shot into the haze.

Captain Rezaian heard none of the warnings,
reported he had reached his first checkpoint.
"Have a nice day," the tower radioed.
A missile blew off the plane's left wing.

Enormous span with engine pod attached,
it fell like Icarus into the sea.
                        On the Montgomery,
crewmen gaped in awe as Zeus rained blood
and fragments of the sky. Turning about
the Vincennes left Iranian waters.

The U.S.
Navy claimed that the warship Vincennes had sped
to defend the Stoval, an unarmed merchant ship.
But that ship, a decoy to lure enemy gunboats
into international waters, was
a simulacrum of radio transmissions,
a Pentagon experiment. The Stoval
existed merely on a computer screen.

IV. Epilogue

Pale against green water, face down, face up,
bodies of women, men, and children float
their quiet screams into the Persian Gulf
past naked Arawaks, thrown overboard
past sailors drowned in long-forgotten wars.
All bodies drowned may pass through the Strait of Hormuz.

Pallas Athena is chasing the Vices:
Avarice, Envy, Sloth, Fraud, and Ignorance
wade in petroleum oil that thickens the sea.
Athena drops her broken spear and doffs
her helmet brimming with golden grain to feed
new life to the dead and to the living, while
she guides their vivid spirits toward the Garden of Virtue
where Vices thrash about in a swamp below
the soaring, rose-topped hedges bordering
the garden and a low, compassionate sky.

Notes

1. A painting (1499-1502) by Andrea Mantegna (1431-1506), from the Musée du Louvre, Paris, shown in an exhibition of his work at the Metropolitan Museum of Art, New York, May 7-July 12, 1992.

2. Hans Koning, *Columbus: His Enterprise; Exploding the Myth* (New York: Monthly Review Press, 1991), 51-53, 57. The information in Section II draws chiefly from this book. Quotations here are from Columbus' log, as they are taken from Friar (later Bishop) Bartolomé de las Casas, *History of the Indies.*

3. John Barry and Roger Charles, "The Vincennes Tragedy: A Sea of Lies," *Newsweek*, July 13, 1992, 28-39. Information in Section III relies heavily on this report; the apt simile here appears on p. 38. A "Nightline" (ABC-TV) account, which included an interview with Captain Rogers, was also useful.

4. "Military theorists write about 'friction,' the inevitability of error, accident, and miscalculation in the stress of combat" (*Newsweek*, 36).

CONVERGENCES

IN NAIROBI

Ah, chorisia,
if there were twenty of you side by side
with all your spines,
and stands of haliconia spread their beaks
like birds of paradise in yellow and red,
and bougainvillea bloomed atop the tallest flame tree,
there still would rise the metal gates
and fences, the sense one must be guarded
behind a screen or double door.

       Day pours its sunlit gardens
on stony streets, the people walking walking.
A barefoot runner pulls a cart of lumber
past women carrying firewood
hunching their shoulders.

Entrance to the City Market swarms with mothers
bearing babies in hungry arms
and a boy huffing
claws at our car window.

In the Tembo curio shop an artist
shows me logs, their bark to be stripped away
to ebony hearts. Bells, masks,
wooden sculptures, Makonde and Maasai,
jewelry and spoons and spears
in silence claim like lions
a pride of recognition,
pride that scales the walls and gates
and blossoms free.

February 26, 1997

LAKE ELEMENTEITA, KENYA

Flamingos cling pink sunlight to the lake
where sacred ibis walk among acacias.
Pelicans in a circle crush and flutter
flap and paddle in unison to confuse
a fish who marvels at the stormy whirl
taunting him upward, hungry to inspect
the busy flash of yellow in turgid green.
Quick pelican ducks to pluck him out of life.

I slip back to my tent to sit with tea
leftover from my daughter's early cup
before her morning birdwalk.

A superb starling, yellow-eyed, unafraid
hops on the rattan table. Plumed
like a gorgeous robin, orange/black
with purple/turquoise iridescence—white
to set it off, he pokes into the sugar,
sips the milk. We are at tea, we two.
Nature, questing nurture, comes to me.

HOLLYWOOD HILLS

1. Vista from Rockledge

Not an unreal vista but a surreal view. By day
the distant mist covers miles in myth
so that you image tomorrow, or past, or even
the present in a manner
spontaneous, untended, like fire
on a hill climbing wildly to shed
its vortex.

Here are palm trees, everything calm. The cat
claws lazily stretching on the hemp doormat. The sun
falls, falls stealthily behind roofs.
Nobody looks. Down there, on the freeway,
somebody else's fires burn somewhere north, locked out of
air-conditioned boxes that roll, whir, whiz and honk,
their tires muttering in low keys, linking direction.
Toward you? Toward mist?
Toward fire?

Houses in these hills, row over row
stagger their pastels upward,
rise from the road above trees
and among them, array
their cubic squares their blank frustrations
against traffic.

Dusk mutes distinctions;
planes echo cars become one motor
mimicking the sound and rush of the sea
unseen behind mist.

Fern trees, palms, and pines connect
the potted greens on terraces to
roots in neighboring soil.

Briefly, my eye holds what I breathe
into my heart.

From smoldering fires night steps forth
lighting another myth
out of the dark.

2. L.A. Light

I keep trying to turn off the lights. But
they're not lights—they're light.
Sunlight. Cloudlight. Metallight
from the highway. Citruslight from trees.
Pinklight caught by plastic shower curtain.
Mirrorlight. The light in me. Light on a cat
lying on a rug, squinting, licking its paws
beside a Christmas tree strung with
old lights and new light.

Four casement windows
overlook sloping clay tiles,
cactus on a ledge,
and the floating city of Los Angeles
entered by highway of hope or escape,
left by the same route.

AMADOU DIALLO

Midnight—a suspect hour
not one day or another
an hour you could be
nice guy/visitor/immigrant/rapist.

And who are these four men in plainclothes
jumping out of an unmarked car and shouting "Freeze?"
They froze you colder than February
but you had identity
in your wallet
you had house keys and a beeper—
did you think they were going to
rob you? Were you thinking that
this was America where nobody would shoot
an unarmed twenty-two-year-old from Guinea who was
nearly an entrepreneur, a street vendor dreaming of owning
his own business, who had his own business on the free
    streets
of a great city, who loved Michael Jordan and the Chicago
    Bulls,
played ball with his cousin and collected wood for the
    evening fire
around which you would sit and study the Qur'an
in your village of Hollande Bouru?
Surprised you were by the bullets,
19 bullets nailing you upright
two officers emptying full clips of 16, nine more of the 41
in on the kill. One breaks into your aorta others assault
your spinal cord lungs liver spleen kidney intestines.
Eleven batter your legs.

"Amadou! Amadou!" cries your mother
who flies from Guinea to weep at the crime scene
in the doorway on Wheeler Avenue.
"Why so many bullets?" asks your uncle.

In Conakry, the capital,
the cabinet meets the plane that carries you home.
Thousands follow you to Hollande Bouru,
where you are buried.

Your family keeps the wooden board
that bore your body.
It stands in a mosque.
Your cousin Mamadou tiles your tomb
next to the grave of your grandfather,
first man in the village
to make a pilgrimage to Mecca.

After the jury absolves the policemen
people protest, get arrested.
Lawyers protest, are arrested.
Schoolchildren protest and are puzzled.
This is not what they learned about justice.
"The trial was for the benefit of the four policemen,"
says Kadiatou, your mother. "Amadou did not
come out here. No one really came to know
who Amadou really was."

Amadou! Amadou!
Her tears course through
a continent. They flush out the bloody stick
shattering the rectum of Abner Louima
batons twirling the body of Rodney King peppered with
taser darts and conducting an orgy of pain.
Tears drown the nightsticks and bullets and stun guns

aiming to subjugate innocent people as if they were
games in a grisly arcade of computerized targets
where heads merely splatter red blobs of light on a screen.
Tears drown the bullets that killed you.
They water the orange groves of Hollande Bouru.

Amadou! Amadou!
The cries run deep into forests and circle the mountains.
They nest among birds in the baobab trees.
They are entering the throats of lions.

LE CHÂTEAU DE LAVIGNY

for C.

In my desktop glass the casement windows
open their blue sky and move white clouds and birds
above the metal roof of the veranda
where plane tree branches tremble every morning
as if the lake were sending special breezes
to rouse their wakeful sensitivity.
The image registering the wind is holding
my face over a manuscript, while above me
and to the left in a ceiling-high cabinet
behind twenty immaculate panes, the twenty-two
Staffordshire dogs are seated in baleful
amazement at all the glazed chintz patterning
the walls, the draperies, bedspreads, headboards, chairs
with bluebirds and finches among the cabbage roses—
a print once chosen with flowers only, draperies
for our first apartment in New York.

You would have liked this place, living in a museum
where you may sit on antique chairs, examine
art and objets, richly satisfied
by authenticity. You would have loved
the iron bull among the cherry trees,
dining on the veranda, entering
conversations about film or listening
to the fields heavy with wheat and sunflowers,
and the hillside weighted with grapes, or seeing a hedgehog
by the wall, and breathing roses, an abundance
you could only wish for in your garden.

Today mist webs between the mountains. Thunder
flung from peaks across the lake roars toward
my room in the Château, past double doors,
empowering torrents of memory pushing through windows
closed to the rain dampening the sills.

CONVERSATION WITH A STONEMASON

I.

The marble squares are perfect. With mallet and chisel you,
Enrique Nava Enedina, sit in the Oaxacan Exhibit Hall, in the
National Museum of Anthropology, Mexico City,
behind a glass screen, as if you are part of the display of
ancient artifacts behind you, the gods, shards, and gargoyles
that peer over your shoulder from shelves.

"Area in Mantenimiento" reads the little white sign on the
    screen.
Area being repaired. On a shelf behind you, description,
of Monte Alban, its apogee in the Seventh Century, its wealth.
Of Mistecan artists who, centuries later, reached their own
    height
of influence and refinement.

II.

On one knee you lean forward. Right hand with mallet handle
tamps the marble into place, left hand holds the square
    steady.
Through the screen you look up at me: alert, head topped
by a mass of slate gray hair, sleeves of your blue workshirt
    rolled back.
The round face of your watch dial shines white against the
    skin of your hand.
A wheelbarrow now rests on the right with a small shovel
    in it,

leans on the freshly mixed cement, a little stack of bricks
    beside it
on the floor. Figures behind you, level with your back,
    emerge now,
almost smiling, quizzical, amused.

III.

The two side panels of the screen move inward to enclose
    you
with six gods on the lowest shelf. You are polishing the
    floor
strewn with empty bags of cement, your workman's cap,
the pail, and an old broom.

Kneeling, you look straight ahead at me. Your brown skin
blends with the stone figures. Your expression repeats
    their expression,
half-satisfied, half-questioning.

Now you are entering the past and they have become
    your present.
It is all about time.

Enrique speaks:

Señora, you visit me again. Each time you stare and write
    in your notebook.
You stare so deeply. I am at work and feel comfortable
    and—
since you are curious—happy among my ancestors from a
    wealthy past.
Never mind my overalls and my labor. I like to work here,

to be with them. Something grand in their presence.
They speak to me. They drop their time into my pockets.

Do not look at me and say, "Poor Enrique. Centuries ago
    his people were rich."
Look at me and say, "Enrique. I know you are a rich man."

*This poem responds to Sharon Lockhart's large triptych of
photographs, taken at the Oaxacan Exhibit Hall, National
Museum of Anthropology, Mexico City, and shown at the Whitney
Biennial Exhibit, New York.*

REQUIESCANT 9/11

September 11, 2001, World Trade Center, Aftermath

1.

Under a hard blue sky
a white shroud rises.

Uptown
air turns acrid.
I close my windows.

Cloud messages
from the plume of hell,
I breathe you, taste the mist—
concrete dust, chairs, shoes,
files, photos, handbags, rings, a doll,
upholstery, breakfast trays,
body parts and parting words
and screams.

Blood of workers, passengers, police—
O firemen running up stairs
past people streaming
from a tower poised to crash—

I breathe you flowing
into the ceaseless sacrifice
of innocents.

My TV exhales frantic images:

Have you seen her? Have you seen him?
Everybody loved her. He was my friend.
Anybody seen them?

Anger rolls over grief and prayers.
"Vengeance!" echoes from toxic caves.

Like spores of a giant fungus,
rage races through the air.
"Vengeance!" the people cry.
All die again.

2. Union Square Park, Two Weeks Later:
   A Pilgrimage

Sunday,
a day as sunny as that other.
Slowly, beneath the trees,
along wire fences garlanding the grass
with flowers, candles, prayers,
love messages on colored papers, photographs,
I walk with vigilant mourners winding past.

Level with branches, George Washington,
astride a horse, carries a fireman's flag
and a peace flag tipped red with a Valentine heart:
"One people."
Invocations anoint his pedestal:
"Love One Another, Give Peace a Chance."

Seated before him on the ground,
Buddhists in unison strike their prayer drums.
Nearby, a couple collect for the Firemen's Fund.
Across the park, pipers and drummers
march past Abraham Lincoln,
proclaim "The Battle Hymn of the Republic."

Later, in a drug store stocked with filter masks
I buy a box. Each one disclaims protection
from toxic dust and poison gas.

Drawn to my City's visible wound
I go downtown.
The subway's nearly empty. I climb
into streets without traffic, buildings powdered white.
Tourists and residents aim their cameras.

On Fulton Street
I join the pilgrimage downhill.

Mask ready, I taste the faintest breath
of acrid smoke, invisible incense
of cries and clamor
still peopling the air.
A woman pulls a suitcase,
a man pulls his.
Which one returns to a ghost apartment,
which one flees?

I reach the crowd and Broadway barricades.
Girders, twisted, wrenched into a pile,
lie helpless beside a jagged crater.
Distant survivor buildings at the rim

face the great square of chaos
a sixteen-acre graveyard. Earth
must have birthed canyons like this,
quaking tectonic rage.

A yellow crane poises high
in homage to the standing shell—
that spire, that Coliseum,
Tower of Pisa leaning grief
against a phantom Twin.

Ground Zero, ground of martyrs, crushed and burned,
their screaming blood bones ashes pulverized
into cement clouds wind carries
through the city to the world.
The crowd, in hushed and rumbling awe,
slows down to get a better view.
 "Keep moving!" a bullhorn shouts.

Into the roiling space
an old sign on a building calls:
A GOOD TIME TO INVEST!

A policeman who had been there from the first
explains to a visitor why people jumped from windows,
those whom a child had witnessed
as birds afire. I wonder if
they'd wildly hoped for flight.

We speak of gratitude.
"I feel the love," he says.

The air falls heavier.
I press a mask against my nose.
My eyes smart a little.
I pass the glass façade of an empty store.
On pedestals, new shoes
display their dust.
A lone pub signals with a scrawl,
"We're Open!"

My skin begins to hurt.
I need to find a subway,
take home
my heartload.

The train shuns regular stops.
At 96th Street
I find a trash can,
throw the mask away.

Epilogue, *Earth Speaks*

You blast omnivorous graves
where millions in memory lie,
you foul my pleasant air,
you level my mountains of ore.

With greed your guiding law,
and vengeance as your creed,
your justice is suspect,
your mercy is select.
All life deserves respect.

Confront the suffering
you mutually inflict.
Share your crusts of bread—
loaves will multiply.
Staunch my terrible wounds
and heal your own thereby.

Let barren hearts accept
seeds from compassionate rain.

Love is the sternest prayer.
All life deserves respect.

Mindful Breathing

*"In the Buddhist tradition, we have the practice of mindful
breathing, of mindful walking, to generate the energy of
mindfulness. It is exactly with that energy of mindfulness that
we can recognize, embrace, and transform our anger. . . ."*
—Thich Nhat Hanh, Riverside Church, September 25, 2001.

I sit by the window,
concentrate on breathing
and become, breath by breath,
a part of breath, drawn
first from this side of the street
bent to shadows dropped
from a scrawny moon.
Now the whole street is breath
flowing uptown
ebbing downtown
to swirl and swirl around
Ground Zero and blur into smoke
from those buried walls and those bodies,
smoke lifting from deep levels
of caves where survivors are hunted
and none can be found,

yet each one remains,
transformed into breath,
a tower, a vortex,
a silent tornado
or a slow wisp of smoke
curling around light bulbs
and the dark pit
of memory

the pit of my stomach that
rejects this air.
It feels natural and wrong to use it
to keep my body intact, unless
each breath be taken in prayer.

I pray for the smoke of Ground Zero
and the smoke over Afghanistan
and every cinder of human history,
I pray that my own breath embrace
the blame and the connections
to wounded and wounding animals
who die, fall, and rise
into the furnace of living.

Lines Composed a Few Miles above St. Paul's Chapel, and beside the Viewing Platform, Ground Zero, July 4, 2002

> *...For I have learned*
> *To look on nature, not as in the hour*
> *Of thoughtless youth; but hearing oftentimes*
> *The still sad music of humanity,*
> *Nor harsh nor grating, though of ample power*
> *To chasten and subdue.*
>
> — William Wordsworth, from "Lines composed a few miles above Tintern Abbey, on revisiting the banks of the Wye during a tour, July 13, 1798"

Towers explode their lives into the churchyard.
Dust stops the clocks and stills the bells,
turns every surface gray, whips through the graves
and crashes a London plane tree against headstones.

Dust storms the church. Emergency workers
wipe ash and blood from their faces, track heavy prints
inside and scuff the pews with boots and belts
where they rest, leave marks "of their ministry,"
as the vicar said, "their sacramental marks."
                                        Emergency!
The Dust weeps, trembling the Great Seal
of the United States presiding from
a wall. Chaos bit by bit subsides
into supplies and food dispensed beneath
the organ gallery—400 meals
each day for workers desperate to find
comrades alive, then grateful to discover
any dead.

                                In the graveyard
spirits kindled in pity rise to accept
the sudden company and wail with them
and weep the world anew. "Has life learned nothing
in two hundred years?" the buried ask,
invite, "Rest here. There's room."
                                "We are innocent!"
the Dust cries, searing the morning air.
                                "Some of us
were soldiers," the buried whisper, "killed for country.
Still, war generates more war." "Where," Dust questions,
 "Where can we ever rest our crush of bones
and concrete, rise from our ruins as we cake
your grass and shake your headstones with our death?"

A graveyard facing the Hudson, among trees.
Behind the sheets rigged to the iron fence:
St. Paul's Chapel, where George and Martha Washington
knelt to pray. (The British—Cornwallis and Howe—
had occupied the pews and knelt there too.)

Handwriting clutches banners hugging the fence.
"We miss you!" "We remember you!" "God bless New York!"

How to reclaim that Nature in which Wordsworth
could hear "a still sad" human "music"
above the roar of bursting engines fueling
pyres of human flesh aflame? Reclaim
a land unpoisoned and unpoisonous,
Nobly conceived?

                                    Pestled into the mortar
of its history, ash from past and present
cross its fields, blur into whirlwinds of its
willfulness, scattered farther, farther from
its heartland.
                              The last time I was here
I stood beside the iron fence, watched workmen
remove top layers of soil to be replaced
with fresh earth and new seeds. Would discards then
be sent to Fresh Kills Landfill's million-ton
debris from the blighted square? Sifted again,
perhaps, as if the ashes might pronounce
their names?

Wordsworth imaged a Hermit sitting alone
by the fire outside his Cave. I see a Country
sitting alone among nations, its eyes
made quiet, not by Harmony
but by a sense of power, itself a Nature
rampant, unconfined, the guide of its own
moral being, self-righteous, self-defined.

Yet there's another presence, interfused
With earth and ocean and the living air.
Call it a Unity of Being—a bond
the poet and the mystic apprehend.
Our dust, our ashes, day and night, the stars,
joy, horror, every foreign tongue—
all grope toward roots that mingle in the dark
while reaching for the light of common life.

Niagara Falls, after Ground Zero

Thundering past green islands
a hundred fifty feet
into the gorge,
river runs
over hard dolomite limestone
and layers of dolomite and shale,
runs as it has run for 12,000 years,
erodes one foot every decade
electrifies the riverbanks
and plunges toward
transfiguration.

People tested
their mettle by your danger.
Sam Patch jumped twice from Goat Island
and survived to die at Genesee Falls.
Annie Telson Taylor, a woman,
was first to go over in a barrel.
Blondin walked a tightrope across.

In 1874, an old schooner,
equipped with three bears and a buffalo,
two foxes and a raccoon,
a dog, a cat, and four geese,
was sent into the current as a stunt.
After the first rapids, two bears
were shot fleeing into Canada.
Terrified animals raced around the deck
spinning over the Falls.
Two geese survived.

White mist rises from you:
hallowed by rainbow,
an ark to Heaven.

On Goat Island,
below the spray
I close my eyes,
try to absorb the falling and rising
into my skin,
into my spirit
where the smoke of Ground Zero
hovers and whispers,
hovers and whispers
in rhythms of blood
meeting
the healing mist
of Nature,
and the permanent witness
of stars.

D. H. Melhem is the daughter of Lebanese immigrants with paternal Greek ancestry. Born and raised in Brooklyn, New York, she earned a B.A. *cum laude* from New York University as a member of Phi Beta Kappa and an M.A. from City College. In 1976 she received a Ph.D. from the City University of New York, which granted her an Alumni Achievement Award in 2001. Her *Notes on 94th Street* (1972) was the first poetry book in English published by an Arab American woman. Manhattan's Upper West Side, where Melhem raised two children, was again her muse for *Children of the House Afire.*

Rest in Love, the acclaimed elegy for her mother, in print since 1975, was reissued in 1995 by Confrontation Press. *Country: An Organic Poem* (Cross-Cultural Communications, 1998), a book-length sequence about the United States, has been called "an American epic." A sequence, *Poems for You* (P & Q Press, 2000), followed as a chapbook. Melhem has won many awards for her poetry. She also wrote a musical drama, *Children of the House Afire,* produced in 1999 at Theater for the New City.

As a scholar, Melhem published *Gwendolyn Brooks: Poetry and the Heroic Voice,* the first comprehensive study of the poet (The University Press of Kentucky, 1987). UPK also issued *Heroism in the New Black Poetry: Introductions and Interviews* (1990), undertaken with a National Endowment for the Humanities Fellowship. It won an American Book Award in 1991. Melhem has written more than fifty essays published in books, critical journals, and periodicals. Her *New York Times Magazine* article on her husband's recovery from a stroke received a New York Heart Association Media Award.

Melhem's novel *Blight* (Riverrun Press, 1995), is distributed by Syracuse University Press. She has read and lectured in venues ranging from cafes, bookstores, and college campuses to Town Hall and the Library of Congress. She serves as vice president of the International Women's Writing Guild. Her web site: http://dhmelhem.home.att.net.

Printed in Canada